"All over this nation, God is stirring the hearts of men to rise up and enter into their God-given destiny. Lou Turner's lifelong passion is to see men enter into their divine purpose in life. 'Living Life God's Way,' of which this book is a part, is born out of this passion. Throughout this Bible study series, Turner opens up God's Word to help you discover HIS plan for your success in your life, family, and work. If you are ready to get off the treadmill, to begin to enjoy God's fullness in your life and make a significant contribution to the world around you, I recommend that you dive into this life-transforming Bible study."

Hal H. Sacks, D.Min., *BridgeBuilders International Leadership Network*

"It seems North American culture is rapidly moving toward what the Bible calls 'everyone doing what is right in his own mind' (Judges 21:25). The prophet Isaiah declared, 'Woe to those who call evil, good, and good, evil' (Isaiah 5:20). This Bible study series will challenge every man in the 21st century as 'iron sharpens iron'! The Q&As at the end of each chapter really personalize the teaching."

Dennis Conner, *Co-Founder/President, Called to Serve Prayer-Coaching Ministry*

"I have known Lou Turner for over twenty years. Lou loves Jesus and has built his life on the Word of God. Lou's Bible study series, 'Living Life God's Way,' is full of biblical truth that has been tested and can be applied by disciples of Jesus in practical ways. These books will help you grow in your faith and gain confidence and competence, which will increase your fruitfulness in Christ.

Mark Buckley, *Founding Pastor of Living Streams Church*

Living Life God's Way

Seeking and Finding God

Lou Turner

Seeking and Finding God
First Edition, 2020
Copyright © 2020 by Lou Turner

Seeking and Finding God is part of the Living Life God's Way Men's Series by Lou Turner.

All rights reserved. No part of this publication may be reproduced, stored in a retrieval system, or transmitted in any form by any means—electronic, mechanical, photocopy, recording, or otherwise—except for brief quotations in critical reviews or articles, without the prior permission of the publisher, except as provided by U.S. copyright law.

Unless otherwise identified, Scripture quotations are from the ESV® Bible (The Holy Bible, English Standard Version®), copyright © 2001 by Crossway, a publishing ministry of Good News Publishers. Used by permission. All rights reserved.

Scriptures marked NKJV are taken from the New King James Version, copyright 1982 by Thomas Nelson. Used by permission. All rights reserved.

Scripture quotations marked (NIV) are taken from the Holy Bible, New International Version®, NIV®. Copyright © 1973, 1978, 1984, 2011 by Biblica, Inc.™ Used by permission of Zondervan. All rights reserved worldwide. www.zondervan.com The "NIV" and "New International Version" are trademarks registered in the United States Patent and Trademark Office by Biblica, Inc.™

Scripture quotations marked (NASB) taken from the NEW AMERICAN STANDARD BIBLE(R), Copyright (C) 1960,1962,1963,1968,1971,1972, 1973,1975,1977,1995 by The Lockman Foundation. Used by permission.

Some of the anecdotal illustrations in this book are true to life and are included with the permission of the persons involved. All other illustrations are composites of real situations, and any resemblance to people living or dead is coincidental.

ISBN: 978-1-7329092-9-8

To order additional books:
www.hislifeinus.com
www.amazon.com

Editorial and Book Packaging: Inspira Literary Solutions, Gig Harbor, WA
Cover Design: MTWdesign, Dickson, TN
Typesetting: PerfecType, Nashville, TN
Printed in the USA by Ingram Spark

He will be like a tree firmly planted by streams of water,
Which yields its fruit in its season
And its leaf does not wither;
And in whatever he does, he prospers.

Psalm 1:3

TABLE OF CONTENTS

Preface   ix

How to Use This Book   xi

Introduction   xiii

1. Finding God   1

2. Men God Used   11

3. Becoming a Man of Prayer   21

4. The Need to Read   33

5. Trials, Tribulations, and Turmoil   49

6. Prayer and Fasting   59

A Final Word   67

About the Author   69

PREFACE

We live in a world that has largely forgotten what manhood is about. In the Western world, men are often portrayed on television as buffoons who are out of touch and must rely on their wives to straighten them out. These characters are portrayed as silly, insensitive, lacking common sense, and when they do speak, they are generally wrong. They are usually portrayed as either ridiculously weak or overly macho. They are not able to commit to a long-term relationship and as a rule mistreat women. Positive role models are hard to find in the media.

However, the Bible teaches a different type of manhood, the authentic one. Men are to be leaders, loving their wives and children, excelling in their work, and standing for truth. They are to be men of wisdom, knowledge, having godly character and seeking after God and His direction. They are to be exhibiting godly leadership at church, in the community, and in business, and to be a light to those around them. They are to be men of compassion and love, as well as courageous and bold when needed.

Men go astray from these ideals, including Christian men, due to improper convictions or beliefs about life. They have received these from various sources: well-meaning family and friends, the media, and the culture around them—a world system that promotes the tearing down of God's biblical truths.

But without proper biblical foundation, we will all go astray.

PREFACE

That's why I wrote these books, containing insights, observations, and biblical truths instilled over the course of my decades of life and ministry. Each booklet is designed to be a stand-alone topic for study and consideration. I hope this series, *Living Life God's Way*, will be used to disciple men in biblical truths for life. Whether you use it for yourself, with a group, or to mentor or disciple someone else, my hope is that it will be a blessing to you and encourage you to seek God and grow in Him.

HOW TO USE THIS BOOK

What does it mean to be a "good" husband and father?
How do I live out the Christian life at work?
What does God want from me—and how am I supposed to find that out?

These were questions that plagued me as a young man—questions, I learned, that are at the front of many men's minds at various times in their lives. For me, these questions began my quest to seek God and discover the answers. My discoveries, over the years of my life, led to this series of booklets, *Living Life God's Way*. The series discusses 13 topics that every man must deal with, regardless of his work, calling, profession, or circumstances. It is difficult to know how to live the Christian life without understanding what God says about these areas of life.

These topics are:

1. Seeking and Finding God
2. Who You Are in Christ
3. A Man's Work and Ministry
4. Understanding Authority
5. A Man and His Wife
6. A Man and His Children
7. Getting Guidance from God

8. Overcoming Strongholds
9. A Man and Money
10. Repentance, Forgiveness, and Restitution
11. Being a Leader
12. A Man and Sex
13. The Test of Pride

You can use these books to study on your own, in a small group, or with a larger group of men. Each topic or booklet is a stand-alone study, and a person can begin with any one he chooses. They are different lengths and can be adapted to various settings—home, church, or community—all topics that are pertinent to today.

Explore what the Bible says about these important and critical areas. The encouragement is to read these with an open heart, asking God to reveal His truth to you in each of these areas of life. Pray that His Spirit will show you His truth, so that you may live in it and enjoy all God has for you. I pray that you experience the blessing and presence of God in your life as you draw closer to Him and more aware of His leading in every area of your life.

INTRODUCTION TO SEEKING AND FINDING GOD

"If there is a God, how do I find Him?"

This is a question many, if not most of us, have had in our lifetime. Seeking God, finding God, and having a meaningful relationship with God are things we should all (hopefully) desire—not just as a one-time event, but in our daily lives. The Bible teaches that we should not only *desire* to have these things, but that they are in indeed ours to have!

Finding God is actually quite simple. However, the journey may have been more complicated and not as linear for those who found God late in life. Thankfully, it is not a requirement to go through an arduous process with multiple steps in order to find God. It comes down to simply accepting what the Bible says, and this well-known scripture sums it up. *"For God so loved the world that He gave His one and only Son, that whoever believes in Him shall not perish but have eternal life"* (John 3:16, NIV).

That's it! You not only find God, but have Him in your life—for your whole life—through His Son, Jesus Christ. And when You commit yourself to Him by accepting His Son, Jesus, with that comes heaven and eternal life. It's a great deal! A heavenly one! If we are sincere, Jesus will come into our life, save us, and begin an intimate and loving relationship with us.

Chapter 1

Finding God

God made finding Him simple so that all who desire can receive. When we accept Christ into our life, the Bible states that He takes up a residence in our spirit. Even if we do not understand at the time exactly what this all means theologically, God will accept our humble sincerity and we can begin a lifelong process of learning about God and getting to know Him.

More often than not, most people begin their relationship with God with many presuppositions, or deeply held beliefs about who they think God is (the older they are, the more likely that is). Some of us may think He's angry, ready to judge and condemn us. Others may believe He is a fickle God whose love is conditional. Some believe He is hard to find and that knowing Him is nearly impossible. However, none of these are true. Pursuing God and getting to know Him is an adventure—the greatest one there is!

The Bible tells us, *". . . anyone who comes to Him must believe that He exists and that He rewards those who earnestly seek Him"* (Hebrews 11:6). That's it. He rewards those who seek Him. He allows them to find Him. But knowing Him and having relationship with Him is a lifelong pursuit, a good one and worthy of our seeking Him.

The Bible states, *"Do not be conformed to this present world, but be transformed by the renewing of your mind, so that you may test and approve what is the will of God—what is good and well-pleasing and perfect"* (Romans 12:2). Without seeking God and reading His Word, our minds cannot be transformed.

The Need to Spend Time with God

If you have been a Christian for very long at all, you have likely heard messages about spending time with the Lord in prayer and Bible study. For those who make this a regular discipline in their lives—to set aside time daily to seek God through Bible reading and prayer—they find that things come up constantly to try to rob them of this time with the Lord. Busyness, lack of sleep, cranky kids, demanding jobs . . . you name it. However, this time is more crucial than you may realize. God wants this time to be meaningful and it is meant to nourish, encourage, and build us up. Yes, we get to spend time with the God of the universe! That's hard for some to grasp, but God intends it to be that way. He desires our time and fellowship with Him.

In my own life, my goal is to get up early each day and spend time in prayer and Bible reading and to be still before the Lord. This allows Him to communicate with me and share any thoughts He wants to impart. This is life-giving and food for my soul. I read His Word, the Bible, and feed on it.

As He feeds my soul and gives me insight, He also teaches me how to live my life and the attitudes I need to maintain. That's why this dedicated time to spend with Him is crucial. It is not just an exercise to do in order to "fulfill a Christian requirement," or another proverbial box to check so we can say to ourselves, "Okay, I've done that, now I can get on with my day." It is a life-giving activity that my heart, soul, and mind desperately need each day. I need the Lord and I need time with Him. Since I am a human being with faults and shortcomings, I need this time with God to learn and grow.

Do I miss it some days due to activities, a busy schedule, or because I allowed the enemy to rob me of it? Yes. But when I come to my senses, so to speak, I realize it and purpose to begin the following day with Him. I must choose to make it a priority in my life and discipline myself to do it, even when I don't feel like it.

Reading and studying God's Word will change and transform you.
If you are a seeker of God and a reader of His Word, you cannot stay the same.
You will change; God will change you.

The Bible teaches us there is a great reward for those who practice this regularly. Psalm 1 says, *"Blessed is the man who does not walk in the counsel of the wicked, or stand in the way of sinners, or sit in the seat of mockers. But his delight is in the law of the Lord, and on his law he meditates day and night. He is like a tree planted by streams of water, which yields its fruit in season and whose leaf does not wither and whatever he does prospers"* (Psalm 1:1-3).

By taking in God's word, thinking about it and its meaning (meditating on it), and determining to apply it to our life, we experience blessing on our life. We grow spiritually. We gain insight and understanding and wisdom. We get wise direction for our life and because of all of this, His divine favor comes on us. As we grow in the Lord, we will begin to fellowship with Him while we go about our day. We get a lot for spending 30 to 60 minutes a day seeking Him. It's a great trade, don't you think?

Of course, we don't just seek Him to get His blessings. Our greatest blessing is Him. We draw closer to Him and our relationship with Him grows.

Getting to Know God through His Word

As we have already covered, the Bible tells us that He rewards us if we earnestly (diligently or consistently) seek Him. That is a great promise worth pursuing. We learn, *"For the Word of God is living and active. Sharper than any double-edged sword, it penetrates even to dividing soul and spirit, joints and marrow; it judges the thoughts and attitudes of the heart. Nothing in all creation is hidden from God's sight. Everything is uncovered and laid bare before the eyes of Him to whom we must give account"* (Hebrews 4:12-13).

We come to realize that the Bible is no ordinary book. It has the ability, through the work of God's Holy Spirit, to penetrate us, deeply to the core of our being. It lays us bare, and judges our thoughts and attitudes. It feeds our souls, builds us up, and teaches us how to live. It teaches us and changes us, directing us how to love our wife, our children, and others. It even gives insight on business decisions and leadership. The Holy Spirit works in us and changes us as we read the Bible with an open heart.

In life, there is nothing more important than seeking God through prayer and Bible study. It is more important than our work and family. Yes, those things are God-given and of great importance. But seeking Him is yet of greater importance so that we can pursue those things in a more meaningful way, His way.

I like what one man said: "In life there are many important things and we should attend to them. But seeking God is more than important, it is vital! We cannot allow the important to rob us of the vital." To accomplish this goal (i.e., to not over-prioritize the "important" and thereby miss out on the "vital"), we need to prioritize and discipline ourselves to seek God. God promises to help us accomplish the important things when we seek Him first.

Prayer

Prayer changes things. Prayer opens up dialogue between us and God. Prayer stirs things in us and makes things happen in the heavenlies. I once heard the saying, "Prayer is the lubrication of the Holy Spirit." As we pray, things begin to happen, whether we see it or not. God responds to our prayers and His Holy Spirit begins to work. Through prayer, we hear from God. Through prayer, we see things change. Through prayer, we change. Through prayer, understanding is given. Through prayer, miracles occur, mountains are moved, people get saved, marriages are restored, families are repaired, and even nations are changed. There is no limit to what prayer can accomplish.

Many times, we do not experience all God has for us because we do not pray enough and seek Him enough. A person who prays will not stay the same. God will change him, use him, and work through him. Do you want to see God work in your life more? Start praying more. God's Spirit will begin to work in your life in a greater way.

If we knew that God Himself wanted us to do something, surely we should want to do that. We can know, with confidence, that God desires us to spend time with Him daily in prayer and Bible study. In fact, the Bible gives many examples of men who practiced seeking God, who were men of prayer, and also tells how God responded to them. We will look at some of these in the next part of this study.

Note: If you have not prayed and asked Christ into your life, and to be your Lord and Savior, this is a great time to do so. We are talking here about having a relationship with God. The way to do that is by becoming His child, and the way to do that is by asking Christ into your life.

All of us must come to a realization that we fall short; we are not perfect. We have all sinned and we all need a Savior. Jesus gave His life to bring us into relationship with Him and God His Father. God is concerned about every aspect, every part of our life. He wants to help us and be a vital part of all we do. He wants to give us direction, wisdom, and help. We just have to invite Him to do so. We do this by accepting Jesus Christ as our Savior and beginning our new life with Him. If you want to accept Jesus Christ into your life, you can pray this prayer: "Jesus, I realize I need You to come into my life and be my Savior. I confess that I have sinned and need You. Please save me; come into my life and be my Lord and Savior."

If you prayed that prayer and were sincere, Jesus has come into your life. You are now His child and He wants to have relationship with you. Your new life in Christ has begun. Now you need to seek Him and grow in your relationship with Him. He has so much for you!

QUESTIONS FOR REFLECTION AND DISCUSSION

1. Looking back on the this chapter and the scriptures mentioned, how would you describe the value of spending time with God regularly?

   _____
   _____
   _____
   _____
   _____

2. What does the Bible say is the role of God's Word (Scripture) in our lives?

   _____
   _____
   _____
   _____
   _____

3. Do you regularly spend time in prayer and Bible reading/study?

   _____
   _____
   _____
   _____
   _____

4. If not, why do you think, in your heart, it is not important enough to discipline yourself to do so? What most regularly keeps you from this practice?

_____
_____
_____
_____
_____

5. How do you think spending time regularly with God will affect your life?

_____
_____
_____
_____
_____

TAKE A KNEE

Let's kneel before the Lord in prayer. If you are not able to kneel physically, then kneel in your heart. *"Dear Lord, please change my heart so I become convinced that seeking You is vital in my life. I realize many things are important, but seeking You is truly paramount. I want to do the important things and not neglect them; help me to prioritize my time so that seeking You and spending time with You is not left out of my day. Thank You for all You have done for me. I praise You for Your goodness to me and Your faithfulness to be with me at all times in my life. Thank You, Father."*

Chapter 2

Two Men Who Sought God

The biblical character of Daniel is one of my heroes. When I read about his life, I am always impressed by his dedication to God. He was born into the royal family of the kingdom of Judah, and then taken captive in Babylon when the Babylonians conquered Israel and Judah. He became an administrator in Babylon and gained prominence in this role (which was the equivalent of his job or work) as he trusted God and sought Him. It is a great story with great life lessons. Please note, he was not a priest (today, that would be a recognized minister), but a man who had responsibility to lead and solve daily problems.

From the outset, Daniel took a brave stand and showed his commitment to God, but did it with wisdom. He and three other Hebrew men were separated from the rest of the captives and put into a special program. Daniel and his friends—Shadrach, Meshach, and Abednego—were to be trained for three years for the king's service. This would afford Daniel and his friends a good life with ample provision if they did well. They would live in royal housing, eat royal food, and be well provided for. However, part of the program was problematic for them: the royal food and wine. Good food and drink sounds good, right? But some of the food they were to eat was forbidden under the Jewish law. Daniel had a tough choice. Compromise, and enjoy the pleasures of the king's food and not risk his potential position, or, obey God, risk losing it all, and leave his future in God's hands.

Have you ever been in that position like that? Go along with the crowd and compromise a bit, which seems to be the safer position to take. Or, determine not to compromise and risk your position, reputation, and future. In Daniel's case, it was only about food. Surely God would understand that Daniel had to eat the king's food, right? After all, God had put Daniel and his friends in the position they were in and surely He wanted them to succeed. Should food cause it all to fail?

Daniel made a difficult decision. He determined he would not eat the royal food because it was forbidden in God's law, the teachings of the Old Testament. However, he acted wisely. He did not get angry and bring an accusation against the king for asking him to eat "unclean" food. The king did not realize the food was unclean to Daniel. He desired Daniel and his friends to be well cared for and healthy, since they were to enter his service.

Daniel realized this, so after some prayer, he appealed to his authority, the chief official in charge of them, and asked if they could be given the food of their choice for ten days. Then, the leaders could determine if Daniel and his friends looked healthy and strong. If so, they asked if they could eat the food of their choosing instead of the king's normal food.

To risk the king's disfavor was a courageous gamble. Nebuchadnezzar, the king, had no problem killing those who opposed or displeased him. However, Daniel realized the goal of the king was for them to be healthy and strong in order to enter his service. So, his appeal was in keeping with the king's desire but in line with his own convictions and religion. Daniel and his friends prayed for favor and they received it. They were allowed to eat the food of their choosing and not violate their law. The Bible relates that, after a 10-day trial period, they looked healthier and stronger than the others in the program and were allowed to continue to eat the food of their choice (Daniel chapter 1).

From that point on, we see Daniel as a man of prayer. The Bible goes on to tell us he prayed three times a day. We do not know how long he prayed each time, but nevertheless, he made it a disciplined practice to do so. He must have felt a need for God's continual guidance in the pagan environment he was in. His dedication was known in the king's court. When Daniel was presented to the king after three years in training, the king found him and his three friends to be exceptional men with great wisdom. The Hebrew men found great favor with the king and entered his service. While Daniel was learning how to serve the earthly king, he was also learning how to serve the heavenly King—God—and to put Him first and trust Him. God gave him great wisdom and insight into his duties and responsibilities.

Daniel's walk with God continued to bring him favor and promotion with three different kings who ruled over Babylon. He was eventually placed in a position over the land as the chief administrator. Here was a man in an ungodly atmosphere, with ungodly people around him who, at times, accused him and tried to get him killed. But God protected him and caused him to rise in prominence and position. If you haven't read his story in Daniel chapters 1 through 6, it is well worth reading. Obviously Daniel's character, his work ethic, his results, and the way he lived his life gained him great favor. God blessed Daniel as he sought Him.

God also gave Daniel the ability to understand dreams, and he interpreted several important dreams for the court, explaining their meaning. He was found to be faithful and competent in all of his duties. At one point, he was falsely accused and thrown to the lion's den, but was unharmed after being in the lion's den all night. This miracle was a sign to the king of the power of Daniel's God. Because of this, Daniel was promoted over all the land. His greatest victory came after his greatest trial! Daniel didn't apologize for his convictions and beliefs. He did not compromise in his seeking God for guidance. We see Hebrews 11:6 played out in Daniel's life: *"(God) is the rewarder of those who earnestly seek Him."*

God used Daniel supernaturally and gave him visions and dreams regarding the future and the end times, which are still prominent in prophetic teachings today (Daniel chapters 7-12). His life was a testimony to all around him. He was given to prayer and seeking God, and God rewarded him by using him in extraordinary ways. He is a great example of a man who sought God, was faithful to Him, and was blessed by God in abundant, ceaseless ways. Not bad for a man in business who was not an official part of the priesthood!

The life lesson? Seeking God pays off. Daniel had some great trials, temptations, and testings, but saw God help him supernaturally through those times. God is always faithful and will see us through all of our difficult times.

David, God's Man and a Great King and Leader

Can you admire a man who is a warrior, a leader, a musician, and accomplishes great things for God? Can a man come from obscurity and humble beginnings and become a great man? Yes, and the Bible speaks of David, who did just that.

David was the youngest of eight brothers. His father owned sheep and David was given the duty of tending the sheep. This was not a sought-after or prominent position by any means. Shepherds often had to sleep in the open country, endure the weather, and guard the sheep no matter what. But being a shepherd gave David time to pursue other things. He became a skilled musician and could play the harp. He also became skilled at using a sling.

David spent much of his alone time seeking God and praying. He established habits of seeking God and being a man of prayer and contemplation. He became a young man of courage and singlehandedly killed a lion and a bear in order to protect his sheep. All the while, his relationship with God grew. God took note of his heart and the fact that he trusted Him and sought Him. In his lowly position, David grew in character and in his faith as he trusted God with his life and listened to His voice.

When it came time for the prophet Samuel to anoint a new king over Israel, he was directed by God to go to the house of Jesse, David's father, to find the next king of Israel. Jesse had some strong, accomplished sons who were also warriors in the king's army. Samuel asked Jesse to have his sons pass before him so that he might discern which one God had chosen to be the next king. When he saw the oldest, Eliab, he thought, *"Surely this is the man the Lord has chosen"* (I Samuel 16:5). Obviously Eliab was an impressive-looking guy! But the Lord spoke something very significant to Samuel in verse 7.

> *"But the Lord said to Samuel, 'Do not consider his appearance or his height, for I have rejected him. The Lord does not look at the things man looks at. Man looks at the outward appearance, but the Lord looks at the heart.'"*

Too often, we focus on what a person accomplishes, their position, their appearance, or their financial status. But God looks at the *heart* of a man—his desire center—to see what that man is really made of. Samuel passed by all of David's older brothers and anointed David as the future king of Israel. His father did not even present him to Samuel to consider, as he was the youngest and only worked in the fields as a shepherd. But God, who looks at the heart, chose David to be the next king. This obscure young shepherd was chosen divinely because of his heart toward God and his character (1 Kings 16).

More of Scripture is spent discussing David's life than any other man except Jesus Himself. His successes and failures are openly displayed as life lessons to us. The thing I personally get from his life is how God greatly used him, blessed him, and was so faithful to lead and guide him throughout his life. David sought God and God responded to him, answering him through all his challenges, difficulties, and trials. We see God protect him, keep him, bless him, and bring His word to pass. We also see God instruct him, discipline him when necessary, forgive him when he repented, and restore him. If you have not read of David's life, I hope you will. It is detailed in 1 and 2 Samuel, 1 Kings, and 1 Chronicles. David was brought up under the Old Testament law with all of its rules and regulations. However, in David we see a man of faith who sought God and had a personal relationship with Him. David went from obscurity to leadership and had great results. He became the most famous king in Israel's history.

In the book of Psalms, written mostly by David, we see him continually talking about seeking God and his relationship with Him. He speaks of his personal trials, his doubts and fears, and the opposition he faced from others. But he also speaks constantly of God's faithfulness and how God helped him, protected him, and brought him through all of the trials and temptations he experienced. He speaks of God's blessings in his life continually.

David truly demonstrated being a man with a living relationship with God. You cannot read the book of Psalms in the Bible without seeing how David was a man of faith who sought God. He speaks of meditating on God's Word daily and practicing its truths in his life. He was truly a man of prayer and one who studied God's Word.

So, can you be a warrior, a poet, a musician, an administrator, a leader, a man of courage, a man who faces doubts and fears, and a man who fails, and yet goes on with God? David was such a man and did all of this. So can you! Regardless of where you start from, God will use you if your heart and life are given to Him.

The life lesson from David's story? Seek God and watch what He does with your life. You may feel obscure and unknown. You may feel that everyone else outshines you—like you are surrounded by people who are "better." But if you seek God and try to please Him, He will see you, hear you, and will respond to you. He will help you, answer your prayers, give you wisdom and insight (James 1:5), and lead you.

David became the man he was because he sought God diligently. Both he and Daniel are two great examples of men whom God used. There are many other stories in the Bible of men who sought God. He was always faithful to respond to them. He will to you also!

The Bible is our teacher. It teaches us how to think, what attitudes to have, and how we are to live. To neglect reading it and embracing its teachings results in missing out on what God has for us. It is like going on a journey and failing to look at our roadmap. We can get lost and experience trouble we could have avoided. Seeking God and His truth brings life to our souls and the direction we need.

QUESTIONS FOR REFLECTION AND DISCUSSION

1. Why were Daniel and David blessed?

2. What about their lives made them different from most men?

3. Are there things you can learn from them to practice in your life? Is so, what are they?

4. Do you believe God wants to do more in your life? Do you believe He wants to use you more? If so, what are some of the things you can do to allow God to work in your life more?

TAKE A KNEE

Let's pray. *"Father, move in my heart to seek You and open my heart to You so You can make me the person You want me to be. Lead me and guide me and show me what You have for me as I seek You. I know You are faithful to answer my prayers and I know this prayer is according to Your will in my life. Thank You that You are a faithful God."*

Chapter 3

Becoming a Man of Prayer

I have read about the lives of many great men who served God and were men of prayer. One in particular impacted me as I read about him and his life: Rees Howells. This man hungered for God and God used him in great ways. Not only did Rees Howells accomplish very noteworthy things, but his influence was felt by many across the world. He impacted people in ministry, business, and government.

Rees Howells was a Welsh coal miner born in 1879, the sixth child in a family of 11 children—eight boys and three girls. His father was employed in the iron works industry and later became a coal miner. After a number of years in the coal mine, his dad started a shoe repair business in the village where they lived. They lived in a small house and had to live frugally. However, the home was full of love and joy that flowed from his parents to the children.

Rees Howells' upbringing had a great influence on him. He was brought up in church, was very religious, and always thought he was a Christian. In his life, he purposed to stay away from things that would be a bad influence on him and that he thought would not be right for a Christian to be involved in.

Rees dropped out of school at 12 and began to work in a tin mill, which required him to be up at 6:00 a.m., and normally not return home until 6:00 p.m. Feeling the need for further education, Rees attended night classes at the village school where he lived. He was a very devoted, religious man and followed his convictions.

This brings up a good point. There are many who accept Christianity and believe in the Bible but have never accepted Christ as their savior. This was true of me. I was brought up in a Christian home and my dad was a pastor of a church. My grandfather was also a pastor as was my wife's dad. Joan and I are both "PKs" or "preacher's kids." I was brought up to believe in God, in Jesus, and in the Bible, for which I am so thankful. After Joan and I were married, we went to church regularly and tried to live Christian lives.

One day, a Christian businessman I knew invited me to have breakfast with him and a pastor who was heavily involved in the lives of businessmen. At this breakfast, the pastor looked at me and asked when I had accepted Christ into my life. I began to tell him of my upbringing, when I was baptized, and my belief in the Bible. After I presented my "good works" and upbringing to him, he asked again when I had become a Christian. When did I accept Christ into my life? I honestly could not remember a time. I remember getting a bit agitated with him as I thought he was questioning my relationship with God, which he was. My pride and self-righteousness were also rising up as he questioned me.

I left that breakfast a bit confused and thinking about what he said. He told me a person is not born a Christian, and does not become one by going to church. At some point, we have to accept Christ for ourselves. Our church and our parents cannot do it for us. It's kind of like getting married. We are not born married, nor do we get married by hanging around married people or hanging around a girl. At some point, to be married, we have to "get married." There is a transaction involved.

Over the next three weeks, I thought about what this man had said. I went from thinking, *Of course I am a Christian!* to trying to remember when I had actually accepted Christ into my life. I was provoked in my spirit and I began to pray for God to reveal Himself to me and make this clear.

One night at about 2:00 am, I woke up and had the clear impression I needed to get up to pray. I went into my office at home, got down on my knees at my desk, and began to pray. It was a supernatural experience. God's Spirit began to lay out for me the plan of salvation in a way that showed me my personal need for Jesus as my savior. I heard Him say to me in my thoughts, "Do you accept this plan for your life?" I said yes and asked Christ to come into my life.

Three weeks later, Joan came to me and asked what had happened to me. There was a change in my life! I shared my experience with her. She was a bit confused. She said, "I thought you were already a Christian." I told her I thought so too and shared the story of the breakfast with the pastor and what had happened in my life. I was definitely a changed person. I went from believing in Christianity and being religious to having a personal relationship with God through Jesus Christ. My life has never been the same.

Rees Howells had a similar experience. One day, a cousin of his asked him a question: "Have you been born again?" This religious and disciplined young man was taken aback by the question. He had never heard the expression "born again" and wasn't sure what it meant. He became defensive and stated he lived a good life and was as good a Christian man as his cousin. He went to church, prayer meetings, and tried to live a Christian life.

His cousin persisted and said, "But do you know you are saved?" Rees was affected by the conversation, and over the next few weeks, he began to wonder. He was reading in the Bible where Jesus told Nicodemus, *"You must be born again"* (John 3:1-18; please read this scripture). He couldn't get away from the thought.

Sometime after this, when Rees was ill, he was contemplating these things, and God's Spirit brought him to a moment of decision. Rees asked Christ to be his savior. His life changed. He went from being a religious man to having a relationship with God.

After he gave his life to Christ, Rees began to pray and seek God daily. God began to lead him in his life and teach him how to live for Him. Over time, he became an instrumental part of great revivals, in which people turned to the Lord and gave their lives to Him. It was not his education or credentials that opened doors to him, but his walk with the Lord. As he prayed and sought God for direction, he would obey the promptings of God's Spirit. He would "pray and obey." This in turn opened doors and he saw God move in response to his obedience. Whole villages were affected by his life as he obeyed God and followed His direction.

Later, Rees started a Bible college where many were trained and sent out in ministry. In a life of faith, he saw God supernaturally supply the funds and material things needed as he obeyed. He bought estates for his Bible school, built buildings, paid salaries of his staff, and influenced people in high positions in the government by praying and seeing God's work. Often, when he believed he was to buy an estate or build buildings, he had no money to do it. He prayed and sought God and God always provided.

Rees prayed for many around him to become saved, and saw many of his prayers answered. He was instrumental in homeless people being saved, attaining jobs, and obtaining homes to live in. He saw entire families saved and transformed as he was moved by God's Spirit to pray for them and believe for their salvation. During World War II, he and his college prayed diligently for the outcome of the war. They were especially impressed to pray for God to intervene at four key points in the war and saw God miraculously answer their prayers.

Learning to Abide

In John 15:7, Jesus made a bold promise to His followers. He told them (and us), *"If you remain in me and my words remain in you, ask whatever you wish, and it will be given you. This is to my Father's glory, that you bear much fruit, showing yourselves to be my disciples"* (NIV). Other translations use the word "abide" for "remain." The Greek word used here is *meno*, which means "to abide, remain, or stay." The verse is saying to remain, abide, and stay in the Lord. It is talking about living a life of fellowship with God.

I have contemplated that verse and its message many times. I have become convinced that the answer to it becoming real in our lives, and our seeing God do greater things in our lives, is in the part of the verse that says, *"If you remain in me and my words remain in you,"* then we can, *"ask whatever you wish, and it will be given you."* It further says *"This is to my Father's glory, that you bear much fruit, showing yourselves to be my disciples."*

When we are abiding in Him, He is putting His desires in us that He wants to fulfill through us. Our heart wants to please Him and we begin to ask Him for the things He desires us to have, and the things He wants to do through us. The emphasis of this verse is our abiding in Him and Him working though us. So, being a channel for God's activity in our life is pleasing to God and brings Him glory. He wants to do it. It brings Him joy!

It goes on to say in verse 9, *"Now remain in my love. If you obey my commands, you will remain in my love, just as I have obeyed my Father's command and remain in his love. I have told you this so that my joy may be in you and that your joy may be complete."* Verse 4 states, *"Remain in me, and I remain in you. No branch can bear fruit by itself; it must remain in the vine. Neither can you bear fruit unless you remain in me."*

Let's take a detailed look at these verses to extract their meaning. (By the way, I hope you will read all of John 15. It is a powerful chapter of Jesus' teachings.) The verses say:

- Remain in Jesus and in His words (strive to obey God and His Word, the Bible).
- Abide in Him and stay attached to him (cling to Him) like a vine to the branch.
- Obey His commands and remain in His love (stay in it, live in it).
- If we do this, we can ask whatever we wish and it will be given to us. We will be asking for those things God has put in our heart to ask Him for, and that are pleasing to Him.
- We will bear much fruit for God.
- God is both pleased and glorified when we bear fruit for Him. He wants to work in us and through us. There is no limit to what He can do through us.
- As we do this, we will experience joy from God in our lives as we see Him work through us.

In 1 John 2:5-6, we find a further explanation: *"But if anyone obeys His Word, God's love is truly made complete in Him. This is how we know we are in Him: Whoever claims to live in him must walk as Jesus did"* (NIV).

Jesus said, *"I tell you the truth, the Son can do nothing by Himself; He can do only what He sees His Father doing, because whatever the Father does the Son also does. For the Father loves the Son and shows Him all He does"* (John 5:19-20, NIV). Jesus abided in His Father, God, and from that flowed the works that He did.

But this again brings up the question, how do we abide in God and do the things He wants us to do? This may sound somewhat difficult, even impossible. How can we abide like Jesus did? He was perfect and always obeyed His Father, God. We are imperfect humans.

However, the Bible does not say we have to be perfect. We will make mistakes on our journey. At times, we will miss the call entirely. But the key is that we keep seeking God. He works through imperfect people. Every person He has ever used was imperfect, including His own disciples and apostles.

Most of us want to see more of God's activity in our life. We want to see God's presence and activity in a greater way. While many may have given up on this, it is God's will to do just that. He wants to be more active in our life and He wants to manifest His presence to us more and more. As we pursue Him and we recognize His activity increasing in our life, His desires become our desires and we begin to ask for His will to be done in us, and it begins to happen. What we are asking for begins to come to pass.

God is committed to help us in this process. He wants to remove those things in our life that are a hindrance to our Christian walk with Him. He wants to heal us, change our thinking, change our hearts, and direct our life. This happens as we seek Him and open ourselves up to His constant working presence. This time of "abiding" with Him, or allowing Him to work in our life and renew our minds, is a daily time with Him, and learning to be sensitive to His leading during our work day.

There are times when I sit down to spend time with Him and my mind is full of things I need to do, or things I am thinking about or concerned about. Sometimes, it takes time for me to be "still" in my spirit and my mind. I begin my time with Him asking Him to speak to me and calm my spirit before Him, so I can have fellowship with Him.

If we are worried, anxious, or have our minds filled with problems or tasks we need to accomplish, it is difficult to be still. Regardless of our circumstances, we can have peace before Him and allow His Spirit to minister to us truth. In this position, not only can God work in us, heal us, and change us, but He can give direction to our lives and lead us to complete His calling. He can give us answers to our problems or direction in our work. He can speak to us about relationships or those things that are burdening us.

If things are especially pressing us or worrisome, it can be difficult to be still and be at peace. But as we choose to trust Him and enter that place of renewed understanding, peace will enter our souls as we give the problem to Him and leave the outcome to Him.

We read in Isaiah 26:3, *"The steadfast of mind You will keep in perfect peace, because he trusts in You."* The word steadfast means; "firmly fixed, not wavering, firmness of mind or purpose," as defined in Webster's Dictionary, 1828 edition. The Hebrew word used here is *samak*. It means hold securely, lay siege to, to rest or sustain. The sense of this word is not wavering, holding on tightly and being able to rest having laid hold of it.

So, to be steadfast means that we choose to trust God in any situation, and we do not let the enemy hassle us or keep us from the peace that comes from trusting Him. As we set our minds on trusting Him, we are steadfast in our resolution and God's rest comes on us as we lean on Him.

Romans 8:6 says it this way: *"For the mind set on the flesh is death, but the mind set on the Spirit is life and peace . . ."* God's

Spirit brings peace to our souls. Galatians 5:22 further says, *"But the fruit of the Spirit is love, joy,* **peace,** *patience, kindness, goodness, faithfulness, gentleness, self-control . . ."*

Peace is a fruit of God's Spirit being in us. If you are a Christian, you are entitled to His peace. We don't have to give in to worry, fear, and doubt. In fact, Jesus said not to. We can trust God with our lives and our circumstances. Easier said than done? Maybe, but God wants us to have the peace we are entitled to.

I have experienced this many, many times. I come to the Lord with my problems and troublesome life situations. Sometimes, I can see no way out and no solution! However, when I choose to trust Him with my circumstances, I immediately feel His peace come over me. What a blessing! I can lay my worries at His feet and believe Him to help me because He said He would, and He is faithful to His word.

Once I took out a loan of several million dollars on a property in order to develop it. We were moving along on it when the downturn of 2006 took place in real estate. The FDIC took over the bank with which I had my loan and froze all of the loans the bank had. At that point, I had over a half-million dollars remaining in the interest reserve on my loan and it was in good standing. The bank defaulted on the loan to me and failed to fund it according to the agreement.

Several years passed by. During that time, we wrote letters asking for payment from the FDIC and asked them to honor the loan. There was no response. One day, I received a phone call from a group that had bought the loan from the FDIC, along with a bundle of other loans. They informed me that they were going to pursue me to pay off the loan. So, the bank defaulted on the loan to me; the FDIC froze the loan and the property, and this group was now going to pursue me legally to pay back the loan. I was going up against the giant of the federal government and the institution acting on its behalf. I lay in bed wondering what I was going to do. (Do you think I was a bit anxious?)

As the days went by and I prayed about this, I came to realize that I could worry and fret or I could trust the Lord and the outcome to Him. I realized I needed to stop worrying, and I needed God's peace to be released in me so I could go about my life with peace and assurance. So, I chose to trust God and give it to Him. When I did, peace came over me. Trusting God led to hope and peace. While I didn't know the outcome, I knew God would help me.

End of the story: it was settled with me having to pay only my legal fees. It went to arbitration and I prevailed. My attorney did a great job and God worked on my behalf. He was faithful. This saga lasted several years from start to finish. I could have developed ulcers, worried, been anxious, been frozen in fear, and, during that time, let it ruin my life. My peace came when I decided to believe God's Word and trust Him with the outcome.

One time, while praying, I felt God speak to me in my thoughts. *I have seen what you can do. Do you want to see what I can do?* All I could say was, "Yes, please." I do want to see God do more in my life. I am still learning and practicing how to practice that in my daily walk.

As we abide in Him, we sense His heart and will for us. The object is not to ask for extravagant material things. But rather, our desire becomes wanting to please Him, as Jesus wanted to please His Father. He gives us desires and reveals His will and what He wants to accomplish in and through us. As we know His mind and His will, we begin to agree with Him and pray for these things to come to pass. God's joy is released in us as we obey Him and do His will.

Trusting and obeying God is not a boring life. It is a life of adventure and excitement as we are challenged to believe God to do things we cannot. We are able to accomplish things beyond ourselves as we follow His leadership. This is true in all parts of our life; in our work, our business, our marriage, our family, our finances, and our relationship with others. We can begin to see things happen supernaturally as God answers our prayers.

Seeking God pays off! It will revolutionize your life! Is your life boring? Are you unfulfilled? Do you want more? Take a step toward God. Seek Him and run after Him. See what He does!

Rees Howells, Daniel, and David were men who sought God and He answered in miraculous ways. They accomplished things way beyond their natural capabilities. So can you.

QUESTIONS FOR REFLECTION AND DISCUSSION

1. We have looked at some examples of men God used in exceptional ways. Do you believe it is possible for you to become a person like that? How would you go about doing that?

   _____

   _____

   _____

   _____

2. Do you believe God wants to work through you to reach others? How do you think He wants you to minister to (serve the needs of) others?

   _____

   _____

3. What are some practical ways you can serve or minister to others?

TAKE A KNEE

"Father, I want to be a person You can use. I want to see Your activity increase in my life. I want to be led by You more and affect others as You work through me. I commit to spending time with You and ask You to draw me into prayer and Bible reading. I ask Your Spirit to open the Scriptures to me and feed me as I read them. Work through me, Lord, and help me to minister to others, to those around me."

Chapter 4

THE NEED TO READ

I have been surprised by the number of men who have told me either they do not read much, or that they don't like to. (Note: I am not referring to men with disabilities that may prevent them from reading.) It is important to know that the Bible itself states we are to read and study it.

"Do your best to present yourself to God as one approved, a workman who does not need to be ashamed and who correctly handles the Word of truth" (2 Timothy 2:15).

"For Ezra had devoted himself to the study and observance of the Law of the Lord, and to teaching its decrees and laws in Israel" (Ezra 7:10).

"Blessed is the man who does not walk in the counsel of the wicked or stand in the way of sinners or sit in the seat of mockers. But his delight in is the law of the Lord, and on his law he meditates day and night. He is like a tree planted by streams of water, which yields

its fruit in season and whose leaf does not wither. Whatever he does prospers" (Psalm 1).

In the 2 Timothy passage above, we read that we need to handle the Word of God accurately. That just is not possible unless we study it! I have seen many get carried away by false doctrine or be deceived, because they were not properly grounded in God's Word. When this is the case, it is easy to be led astray.

Ezra, a leader of Israel, devoted himself to the study of the Law in the Old Testament, the part of the Scriptures available to him at that time. He wanted to be careful not to lead others astray and to live a life in observance of the law, so he could please the Lord.

David wrote in Psalm 1 that the person who studies the Word and meditates on it (thinks about it and applies it to his or her life), will be blessed by God and his or her work will prosper. God tells us to read and study the Bible, and there is a reason; He wants us to live a blessed life and not be led astray. David said he meditated on it day and night. He wanted to please God with his life and live according to Biblical truth.

In addition to the Bible, I regularly read other books by those who follow the Lord. I have gained great insights from others writings that have helped me and blessed me. Of course, I always make sure the writings agree with God's Word. Because others seek God and get insights from their study and walk with God, what they have to share can bless us. It is true not everything written is worth reading or agrees with God's Word, but I have been blessed by authors who have a sincere heart, seek God for His leadership, and study His Word.

We just can't take the position that we "don't like to read." If that is where you are, I want to encourage you to ask the Lord to change your heart and give you a desire to read and study His Word. I also want to encourage you to begin to discipline yourself to set aside time daily to read the Bible and pray. We just can't grow spiritually the way God wants us to unless we make this a discipline in our life. If there is a reason for reading to be an obstacle for you, consider listening to the Bible on tape and other books by Christian authors.

The same can be said for all the other disciplines in our life: what we watch, what we eat, whom we spend our time with, and what we read. What we take in with our eyes and our ears has a profound effect on our hearts and minds. We need to feast on good things, not junk.

Jim was a man I knew who was in the same basic profession I am, building. He professed Christ as his savior and went to a good Bible-believing church. As I spent time with Jim and learned more about him, I discovered he was a football fanatic. Yes, he was hooked on it big time. He would watch Monday night football, Thursday night football, and every game he could watch on Sunday. And then there was college football all day Saturday.

I asked him once about his life with the Lord and how much time he spent praying and reading God's Word. He told me he did not have time in the mornings to just sit and read and pray. But instead, he would pray as he drove. So, even though he spent 10-15 hours a week watching football (or more), he did not have any time to devote alone with God. Doesn't this seem a little off to you?

As time went on, I began to get burdened for this man. As I prayed for him one morning, I got the distinct impression that if he did not change his priorities, he would lose his marriage and business.

The next time we were together, I told him I had been praying for him and that I had received the impression that if he did not begin to spend more time with his family and with God, he could lose his family and his business. He told me that all was well with his family, and I had no reason to be concerned about that. His attitude was basically that I should mind my own business and leave him alone. Two years later, his wife left him and he went bankrupt. I believe this could have been avoided if he had sought God and changed his life.

Many Christian men and women do not take the time to seek God regularly and encounter difficulty and hardships because of it. They make bad decisions, use their time unwisely, and their life suffers. I am not saying that those who do seek the Lord will not have times of adversity or difficulty. However, those who do not will suffer things they should not have suffered had they been grounded in God's Word. The Bible clearly promises direction from God as we ask for it and His help in all areas of our life:

"If any of you lacks wisdom, he should ask God, who gives generously to all without finding fault, and it will be given to him" (James 1:5).

"Trust in the Lord with all your heart and lean not on your own understanding: in all your ways acknowledge Him, and He will make your paths straight" (Proverbs 3:5-6).

My purpose is not to condemn or even be critical of those who do not practice daily prayer and Bible reading, but to encourage everyone to do so! If this is you, you are missing out on many blessings for your life and growing in your relationship with God.

Being Transformed

Being transformed is a tremendous benefit of the "new life" that is ours through our faith in Jesus Christ. In 2 Corinthians 5:17, we read, *"Therefore, if anyone is in Christ, he is a new creation. The old has passed away; behold, the new has come."* Some call it being "sanctified," or changed.

The word "sanctify" is an important one in Scripture. In the Old Testament, the Hebrew word for it is *qadash*, which means to be set apart for holy use. In Old Testament times, this kind of "setting apart" included practices such as the sacrifice of a sheep or bull under the Old Testament sacrificial system. It happened all at once, as the animal was selected, for a holy purpose. But the word also has another meaning, which meant something purified or consecrated. This meaning referred to a continual process, one that happens over time.

In the New Testament, the Greek word used for this concept is *hagiazo*, which means "to make holy, to consecrate or to sanctify." Another meaning of this word would be to purify or prepare for divine service.

Sanctification can be said to happen at salvation as we are made clean and set aside for God. It can also be said to happen when a person makes a commitment to follow God in a greater way and sanctifies himself for the Lord's purposes. It is also a process that continues all of our life as we are changed, purified, and continually prepared for God's service as we live out the Christian life. Obviously, when we first become Christians, we do not know as much as when we have sought the Lord for years. As we seek God and yield to His work in us, we continually change and become transformed into the person He desires us to be. This is sanctification.

The Bible tells us, *"Do not conform any longer to the pattern of this world, but be transformed by the renewing of your mind. Then you will be able to test and approve what God's will is-His good, pleasing and perfect will"* (Romans 12:2). This transformation process helps us recognize and distance ourselves from the world's way of thinking and living contrary to God's will. It supernaturally shifts us into His path of truth for our lives.

The word "transform" is another important word. It comes from the Greek word *metallasso*, which means to "exchange for" or "to change." It is related to the word "repent," which means "to change one's mind or purpose."

So, to be transformed means to change our thinking and change our life. We become *"qadashed"* or sanctified as we do this. We get closer to God and thus are purified and made more like Christ. In doing this, He can use us and demonstrate His life and love through us more and more. Our relationship with Him grows through this process and throughout our lifetime. As we grow, we throw off the things that can hurt or hinder our life. Wrong thinking changes. Emotional wounds are healed. The truth enlightens us and changes the way we live our life. We are transformed!

That being said, God can (and does) use us the moment we become a Christian to reach others and proclaim His truth. We should not discount God's use of us from the moment we are saved or become Christians.

In Mark 5, Jesus encountered a demon-possessed man. The man was living alone in the tombs of that region, causing great fear and concern to the locals. He was so bound by demons that he could break the chains when they attempted to subdue him. When he came into Jesus' presence, Jesus delivered and cleansed him. He was radically changed and desired to go with the Lord.

But Jesus told him to remain where he was, and to tell his family and the people in the area what God had done for him, how he was delivered and transformed. As he began to do so, the people were amazed (Mark 5:1-20).

God began to immediately use the formerly demon-possessed man to proclaim the goodness of God and to affect others with his testimony. In the same way, God can use us all from the moment we become saved. However, this does not mean that God does not want us to grow spiritually. The Bible gives many examples of God preparing men and women for a greater use, even though they had a heart for Him early on in their walk of faith.

The same is true for us. When we become a Christian, we should want to share all God has done for us. He can begin to use us immediately. But we must also seek God for all He has for us. We need to be "transformed" by having our mind renewed. As we are transformed, our thinking will change, our life will change, and our habits will change.

Science Supports Our Need to Slow Down and Reflect

Current research shows that there is a great need for us to slow down and have regular times of reflection, or mental rest, where we think on the truth and allow it to have positive impact on us. Dr. Caroline Leaf, a Christian PhD who has worked in the area of cognitive neuroscience since 1985, states some rather groundbreaking things in her book, *Switch on Your Brain*. She states that the way we think of ourselves, and the things we believe to be true, have a great impact on us. It actually has an effect on our brain and the way it functions, as well as our emotions and our behavior.

Dr. Leaf explains that when we do not enter into a disciplined and self-reflective pattern of thinking on the truth, but instead dwell on things that are negative for our life, it can cause us to experience poor self-esteem, depression, worry, anxiety, and health issues. It can cause us to have memory issues, fuzzy thinking, and many other manifestations, including neuropsychiatric disorders.

Our brain responds with healthy patterns, circuits, and neurochemicals when we think deeply on positive things and not just skim the surface of multiple pieces of information. Many just want quick "sound bites" or summaries of information. But the benefit comes when we take the time to think on positive, truthful things and let them sink into our heart and mind.

Dr. Leaf further explains that when you go over something—reading it and thinking about it—then write it down and repeat the process, you deepen your knowledge and understanding. Doing this even causes physical growth in your brain!

Most of have thought that whatever IQ or intelligence we were born with is what we get for life. However, in her research, Dr Leaf has shown that our IQ can increase, as well as our mental abilities to focus and learn.

When I went to college, I remember at times I could actually read four to five pages in a textbook and at the end, tell you very little of what I had read. My mind would wander and I had trouble focusing and retaining. Then, a number of years ago, I felt God leading me to begin to memorize and meditate on larger portions of Scripture, whole chapters at a time. I did this for a period of time and noticed that not only did I learn much more deeply what God's Word had to say, but my ability to concentrate, focus, and learn had greatly improved. Not only did I have a much greater understanding of the truths and teachings of the Bible, but my mental abilities seemed to grow. My mind and emotions were being healed and my life was benefitting from it. My walk with God grew and my life was changed by the greater understanding I had of the truth of God's Word.

I know what the Bible says is true: *"For the Word of God is living and active. Sharper than any double-edged sword, it penetrates even to dividing soul and spirit, joints and marrow; it judges the thoughts and attitudes of the heart. Nothing in all creation is hidden from God's sight. Everything is uncovered and laid bare before the eyes of him to whom we must give account"* (Hebrews 4:12-13).

God's Word penetrates us as we study and meditate on it. It heals our life and our souls. It brings life to us, His life. It illuminates us, leads us, and guides us. It makes us more sensitive to His Spirit so that we can hear what He is saying to us.

God wants to fill us with His Word and His Spirit so that we can live our lives for Him and accomplish all He has for us. This simply cannot happen unless we discipline ourselves to seek God regularly. He responds to our seeking Him.

As we seek Him, He rewards us with His presence, His wisdom, and His leading. The verse we have previously discussed—*"Anyone who comes to Him must believe that He exists and that He rewards those who earnestly seek Him"* (Hebrews 11:6, NIV)—is important. Seeking God is a win-win for us with no downside—only an upside.

Do you want your life to change? Do you want greater meaning, fulfillment, and greater activity of God in your life? You can have it. Seek God and ask Him to be more active in your life. He wants to! He wants to show you His will for your life. He wants to transform our relationships, our marriage, our children, our work life, our health, our finances, and the way we live our life.

Getting to Know God

We have talked about finding God, but there is an aspect of seeking God that involves getting to know Him. It doesn't happen all at once. But it can happen over time as we seek Him. One of my favorite stories that illustrates this is about Moses.

Moses was leading the children of Israel through the wilderness to the Promised Land, the current land of Israel. The children of Israel were over two million people strong and leading them was a daunting task. They were a stubborn and rebellious people, and when God did something miraculous among them, they praised Him for it. But when things did not go their way, they complained and murmured against Moses and against the Lord.

The trials Moses went through leading this group caused him to long for more of God's presence. At one point, he cried out to God to reveal Himself, to allow Moses to visually *see* Him. I am not sure of exactly why Moses felt this need. However, his responsibility was great, and he knew God had called him to carry out this huge job. In his heart, he must have felt inadequate for the task and felt he needed more of God. He wanted to be in God's presence and actually "see" Him. He longed to know God more.

There are few men who knew God as Moses did. But he wanted more, he needed more, and he asked for more. Let's pick up the story in Exodus chapter 34, verses 5-7: *"Then the Lord came down in the cloud and stood there with him and proclaimed His name, the Lord. 'The Lord, the Lord, the compassionate and gracious God, slow to anger, abounding in love and faithfulness, maintaining love to thousands, and forgiving wickedness, rebellion and sin. Yet He does not leave the guilty unpunished; He punishes the children and their children for the sin of the fathers to the third and fourth generation.'"*

How did God reveal Himself to Moses? He revealed His character, the person He was. Moses cried out to God to know Him and God revealed Himself to Moses by telling Him about His nature. In reading this, we need to grasp what God said about Himself.

God says He is a compassionate God. He is gracious and slow to anger. He abounds in love and faithfulness. He maintains His love and forgives wickedness, rebellion, and sin.

Wow, what a God. I want to know Him more in my life. God's description of Himself shows us He is the God we all desire. He is patient with us. He loves us. He forgives us. He is slow to anger. He ***abounds*** in love and faithfulness. And, as we seek God, He reveals Himself to us and we come to know Him greater.

That does not mean we never struggle or waver. Sometimes we get outright attacked! Satan works to try to keep us from truly knowing Him. He lies to us and tells us God is not like this. But as we go back to God, He reveals Himself once more as a loving, forgiving, and compassionate God.

To know God's nature is to know Him. In Heaven, we shall see Him and dwell in His very presence. But on Earth, we cannot see Him, so He reveals His nature to us.

Becoming a "Tree of Life"

In the book of Genesis, it speaks of the Garden of Eden where Adam and Eve began their lives. In the garden, there were two trees the Bible speaks about: the "Tree of the Knowledge of Good and Evil," and the "Tree of Life" (Genesis chapters 2 and 3). The Lord told Adam and Eve not to eat of the Tree of the Knowledge of Good and Evil, and said the day they did that they would die. But Satan tempted them, and what do you know? They ate of the tree, and death came upon them and their world. Their sin brought the consequences of sin into the world, one of which was death. While they did not die right away, death did enter the world at that moment and eventually they passed on. Had they not sinned, they would have lived forever in the garden in fellowship with God.

Most Christians have heard the story, but the tree that is not taught about much is the Tree of Life. This tree is a representation of Jesus Christ, the life giver. The Tree of Life disappears when Adam and Eve were driven from the Garden of Eden. However, it appears again in the Book of Revelation.

> "*Then the angel showed me the river of the water of life, flowing from the throne of God and of the Lamb down the middle of the great street of the city. On each side of the river*

stood the Tree of Life, bearing twelve crops of fruit, yielding its fruit every month. And the leaves of the tree are for the healing of the nations. No longer will there be any curse. The throne of God and of the Lamb will be in the city, and His servants will serve Him. They will see His face, and His name will be on their foreheads" (Revelation 22:1-4).

The Bible speaks of Jesus, who redeemed us from sin and all curses, being the "water" of life and the "tree" of life. He is the life-giver. So, while the river of life and the Tree of Life will have practical purposes in heaven, they represent the work of Jesus in the world.

We have the choice of what type of tree we want to be. The Tree of the Knowledge of Good and Evil represents the consequences of knowing sin. Preaching "right and wrong" alone does not change people. They need the "life-giver" or the Tree of Life in their life.

In our own lives, our eyes can be opened to further understanding of either righteousness or sin. If we participate in sin, we will become knowledgeable about it. If we choose righteousness, we will become knowledgeable about God and truth.

"Do you not know that when you present yourselves to someone as slaves for obedience, you are slaves of the one whom you obey, either of sin resulting in death, or of obedience resulting in righteousness? But thanks be to God that though you were slaves of sin, you became obedient from the heart to that form of teaching to which you were committed, and having been freed from sin, you became slaves of righteousness" (Romans 6:16-18, NASB).

Paul, the author of Romans, is speaking about our becoming bound to whatever we give ourselves over to, either sin or righteousness. Obviously, we want to give ourselves over to righteousness and experience all Christ has for us.

In life, if we focus on knowing God and living for Him, life and truth will flow out of us and we will become life givers, or trees of life, to others around us. That is what we want to be and is our ultimate calling as believers—to be "Trees of Life." We want to be life-giving to our families, neighbors, coworkers, employees, and beyond.

We can have knowledge about the Bible, know about "right and wrong," and be religious and legalistic. We can point out what is wrong with people, tell them all about their sin and their wrongdoing, and bring condemnation on them. Or, we can share the truth with them in a life-giving manner. We can bring Jesus to them, loving them to health and healing. We can build them up and encourage them, or, we can pile judgement on top of them, making them feel worthless. Those are our choices: we can be a *"Tree of Life,"* or a *"Tree of the Knowledge of Good and Evil."*

Yes, we need to know right from wrong. But the knowledge of right and wrong doesn't save people. What saves them is giving them hope for their life and leading them to The Hope, Jesus, who wants to save, redeem, and heal them.

The Healing of Our Soul

The Bible speaks of our need to be healed emotionally. Some people have had devastating things happen to them such as sexual, emotional, and physical abuse, that has left them hurt and wounded. In some way or another, our souls are in need of healing. For purposes of this study, I am defining the soul as our mind, will, and emotions. It is our inner being, the person we are.

The Bible speaks of the desire of God to heal us and make us whole in our souls. Consider these passages:

"The Lord is near to the brokenhearted and saves those who are crushed in spirit" (Psalm 34:18, NASB).

"He heals the brokenhearted and binds up their wounds" (Psalm 147:3, NASB).

"The Spirit of the Lord God is upon me, because the Lord has anointed me to bring good news to the afflicted; He has sent me to bind up the brokenhearted, to proclaim liberty to captives and freedom to prisoners; to proclaim the favorable year of the Lord and the day of vengeance of our God; to comfort all who mourn, to grant those who mourn in Zion, giving them a garland instead of ashes, the oil of gladness instead of mourning, the mantel of praise instead of a spirit of fainting. So they will be called oaks of righteousness, the planting of the Lord, that He may be glorified" (Isaiah 61:1-3, NASB).

It is clear from these verses that the Lord both knows of our past hurts and wounds and wants to heal us of them. He wants us to experience joy, peace, and have a mouthful of praise because of the things He has done for us. Healing of our inner person happens over time as we allow God to work in our life. This is another reason why it is so important we spend time seeking God. The Bible says, *"Draw near to God and He will draw near to you"* (James 4:8, NASB).

God promises to reveal Himself to us as we draw close to Him. He will minister to our wounds and hurts and heal us from the inside out. For those who are deeply wounded, that might seem like a dream that cannot come true. But God is both able and willing to meet our needs and bring healing to our souls, even the deepest, darkest parts. We need to talk to God about our hurts and wounds and ask Him to heal us. Remember, it is always okay to ask for help. If needed, consider seeking prayer and counsel from a wise, godly believer in your life.

All of us need to be renewed in our souls. Some just have greater needs than others. But we are all needy of God. Let Him show you what He has for you. His plan for us is greater than we are able to accomplish on our own. And He is faithful to bring it to pass.

QUESTIONS FOR REFLECTION AND DISCUSSION

1. Are you a person who doesn't read much and tells yourself you just don't like to read?

    If so, are you willing to ask God to change your heart and begin to read His Word and other books that can bless you and build you up? How might you start?

    _____

    _____

    _____

    _____

2. What are the ideal daily times where you can slow down and think on the truths the Bible shares about God and about you? Are you willing to begin to do this if you are not already doing it? What might this look like for you?

    _____

    _____

    _____

    _____

3. Have you ever been a "Tree of the Knowledge of Good and Evil" instead of a "Tree of Life"? Whom can you begin to encourage and build up?

_____

_____

_____

_____

4. Do you feel you have emotional wounds that need to be healed as part of your new life in Christ? List below the areas where you think God wants to heal you, and wants you to begin to seek Him through prayer for this healing.

_____

_____

_____

_____

TAKE A KNEE

Dear Father, I realize You are the giver of life and hope. You desire to heal me, build me up, and use me to encourage others. Come now and heal my soul of dashed hopes, of fears, of past wounds and discouragement, and reveal to me Your desire to love me and build me up. Show me You are my healer and restorer. I confess I need You, Lord, to do this in my life. I am needy and You are the giver of all I need. Thank You for Your love, forgiveness, and for being the healer of my soul."

Chapter 5

TRIALS, TRIBULATIONS, AND TURMOIL

F inding God in the midst of trying times can be difficult. None of us like trials, tribulations, or turmoil in our life. Of course not! But in this life, we will all experience them. Some people handle these times better than others. God wants us to have understanding so we will know what to do and how to pray when we encounter adversity. Let's look at a few reasons why we may go through difficult times.

Satanic Attack

"Finally, be strong in the Lord and in His mighty power. Put on the full armor of God so that you can take your stand against the devil's schemes. For our struggle is not against flesh and blood, but against the rulers, against the authorities, against the powers of this dark world and against the

spiritual forces of evil in the heavenly realms" (Ephesians 6:10-12, NIV).

Many of us are familiar with this verse of Scripture but do not think about it or consider it very often. The truth is that, on planet Earth, there is a war being fought for the souls of men, women, and children. The war is all around us and we are in it. We are to bring the light and truth to those around us for them to be set free and we are to defeat the works of Satan as the Lord leads us.

All you have to do is listen to the news, watch TV, read the newspaper, and listen to many of the conversations of people around us to realize that Satan and his followers are working to entrap people, destroy lives, and lead people astray. He does not want people to follow God and walk in His truth.

Satan likes to work in stealth mode. He does not want us to recognize his work. Rather, he wants us to believe the worst about ourselves, about others, and even believe he is too powerful to defeat. However, the Bible teaches us that Jesus defeated him through the work He accomplished on the cross. Now, through Jesus Christ, we have the power and ability to defeat Satan's works in and around us. God works through people, and He wants to work through you.

Satan will put thoughts into our minds to disturb us and rob us of our peace. Satan cannot read our minds as some might think, but he can put thoughts there. He will give us reasons to worry, fear, feel inadequate or insecure, be overcome with doubt, experience lustful thoughts, have greedy thoughts, want to give up, and doubt God's goodness and love for us, just to name a few. He is a very real enemy and wants to bring havoc into our lives and rob us of our peace. Often we come under attack and do not realize it is Satan and his forces that are harassing us.

I have been surprised how often negative thoughts have come to me about things that have never even happened. For example, at times I have thought that people were speaking ill of me, despite a lack of evidence, only later to discover that my thoughts were wrong. I got upset for nothing! At other times, I have thought negative thoughts about others, becoming angry and feeling the need to "straighten them out," to later discover I was wrong, or that their motivations were much different than I imagined. I call these types of thoughts "vain imaginings." We imagine and think on things that are not true, and it causes us to be distraught and fretful. These are harassing thoughts from Satan or his followers. He is called the "accuser" for good reason!

By the way, the Bible calls Satan's followers demons and seducing spirits. Their goal is to overcome us if we allow them to. They want to lead us astray, and to seduce us to enter into sin. That's the key: our allowing them to. It is very important that we do not allow these negative or seducing thoughts to stay in our mind. The Bible tells us, *"Whatever is true, whatever is noble, whatever is right, whatever is pure, whatever is lovely, whatever is admirable—if anything is excellent or praiseworthy-think about such things. Whatever you have learned or received or heard from me, or seen in me—put into practice. And the God of peace will be with you"* (Philippians 4:8-9).

This is not just a good suggestion, but a real and necessary life practice if we are to have peace. We just cannot allow ourselves to think on things that are going to negatively impact our lives. When we allow ourselves to think on things that are harmful to us, or practice gossiping or slandering others (speaking badly about them), it gets into our hearts and takes root.

> *"When tempted, no one should say, 'God is tempting me'. For God cannot be tempted by evil, nor does He tempt anyone; but each one is tempted when, by his own evil desire, he is*

dragged away and enticed. Then after desire has conceived, it gives birth to sin; and sin, when it is full-grown, gives birth to death. Don't be deceived, my dear brothers. Every good and perfect gift is from above, coming down from the Father of the heavenly lights, who does not change like shifting shadows" (James 1:13-16).

Satan wants to "drag us away" from our path by distracting us with sinful thoughts and enticing us. When we give into them and allow them to enter our hearts, they take root and give birth to sin—that is, wrong thoughts or actions.

Guarding what we think affects us greatly—in a positive way. It affects our walk with God and our relationships with others. It also affects our hearts, minds, and emotions. The Bible tells us that Satan is our accuser (Revelation 12:10). He accuses us before God, accuses others to us, and also accuses us to ourselves. He tells us we are no good, unable, and unworthy. But our worthiness is not in ourselves, it is in Jesus who saved us and redeemed us! We stand clean before God by the work of Jesus and our faith in Him as our Savior. We are saved and cleansed. We have become a new creature, and we stand before God innocent, whole, and pure through Jesus. What a glorious truth! Even though we make mistakes, our life in Jesus does not change. We are still His child and are "in Christ." We have been washed whiter than snow!

Satan's attacks can bring discouragement, disillusionment, and depression. I believe much of the depression we suffer is simply spiritual attack. We lose our hope, which causes us to lose our trust in God to help us. We focus on ourselves and our circumstances, and because of all of this, our faith is replaced by doubt. We end up discouraged and down. That's what Satan wants us to be—discouraged and low in faith. What we think, and what we allow ourselves to dwell upon mentally, can have a real impact on us.

So it is important, when we feel we are under attack, to stand against Satan, reject wrong thinking, and trust God. This trust will lead us to peace and victory over Satan's attacks.

Bad Decisions and Seeking God for Help

When we make bad decisions, consequences follow. Trust me, I know. I have made a lot of bad decisions that I have had to work through. Often, we don't realize that what we are struggling against is the result of a bad decision, especially if we are still trying to convince ourselves it was the right decision.

In Genesis 16, Abraham and Sarah made a bad decision. God had promised them a son and, by all standards, they were running out of time. Sarah became desperate and offered her handmaid to Abraham to gain a child, hoping for a son. This was a common practice in those times. Not something we should do today!

Sarah's maid, Hagar, became pregnant and gave Abraham a son. But that was not God's plan and the circumstances that followed affected Abraham and his descendants for thousands of years (and still affect them even today). God eventually gave Abraham and Sarah the son He had promised but they had to deal with the consequences of the son through Hagar.

We will all make bad decisions. Some are minor and when we realize it and change direction, it clears it up. However, others have more far-reaching effects. We must always be willing to work through the consequences, and at times it's painful.

However, God is gracious, kind, and forgiving. When we realize we have made a bad decision and confess it to God and ask for His help, His grace comes upon us and the situation, and He begins to help us. Some situations work out quickly and some take time. But God is there to help us through it and will do so. The Bible says, *"God is our refuge and strength, an ever present help in trouble. Therefore we will not fear . . .* " (Psalms 46:1-2). God is always with us and will help us as we cry out to Him.

In 2 Samuel 21, there is a story about how the nation of Israel was suffering under a famine for three years. David, the king, began to seek God to see what could be done to end the famine. God spoke to David and revealed to him that the land was suffering because Israel had broken its covenant with the Gibeonites (Joshua chapter 9)—a bad decision. David repented on behalf of the kingdom and went to the Gibeonites to repair the damage done in their covenant with them. Afterwards, the famine broke.

There are times God is trying to get a message to us and we may be experiencing resistance or difficulty because we need to hear from God and get into alignment with Him. We will only know this if we pray and seek God until He enlightens us about our circumstances and we obey the direction He gives us.

We may have a problem with anger, with a critical spirit, with gossip or slander, neglecting our family, or any number of things God is concerned about and wants to communicate with us about. Or, we may have made a bad decision and need to turn it around. When we don't listen, He may have to turn up the heat a bit to get our attention.

God wants to get our attention and renew us from the inside out so we can have a richer, fuller life with Him. He wants us to learn and grow—not become stagnant or mired in our problems.

Let yourself really consider if there are any areas where you've made bad decisions or are out of alignment with God's will. Are you neglecting your family? Are you neglecting your relationship with God? Are you neglecting your wife? Have you been deceptive with others? Do you have a problem with applying yourself in your work? Are you living an area of your life not according to Scripture? Is there anything else the Holy Spirit may be speaking to you about in your life?

God is committed to changing us and making us better, from the time we accept Christ as our savior until the day we die. He is faithful to reveal to us whatever it is we need to know and understand. When we are not seeking God and asking for understanding, we may not know the reason we are experiencing trials and troubles. However, God wants us to understand and learn from Him. He promises in James 1:5 that if we lack wisdom, He will willingly grant it. He wants to build us up and bless our lives.

How God Works to Change Your Heart

Some things in our life cannot change unless there is first a change in our hearts.

Saul was a zealous man. He was a follower of the Mosaic law and rigid in his beliefs. He was a leader in the religious sect called the Pharisees in Israel. He believed that Christians, followers of Christ, and were leading the Jewish people astray and away from the law they were to follow. He was so convinced of this that he obtained authority from the Jewish leaders to persecute and imprison Christians. He was a man on a mission and his mission was to do away with Christianity.

On his way to Damascus, Saul had an encounter with God. Jesus appeared to him supernaturally and told him he was in error. He was blinded by the light coming from Jesus and was blind for several days. During this time, he had time to reflect on his actions and his encounter with God.

After three days, God sent a man named Ananias to pray for Saul to receive his sight again. He was healed of his blindness and this encounter changed him. His heart was changed and he went from being a persecutor of the church to declaring to all that Jesus was the way to God. He was so changed that God changed his name from Saul to Paul to signify his new life. His encounter with God not only changed his heart, it changed his entire life (Acts 9).

We all come into adult life with many expectations and dreams. Many of these may be good and right, and some may be wrong for us. Our heart attitudes may include a critical spirit, a callousness toward others, the inability to show love and affection, taking others for granted, or driving desires that can get out of control or become unbalanced. Often, these are blind spots in our life. For change to take place, we need a change of heart.

God works on us in many ways, but His ultimate goal is to make us more like Christ, our example of perfection. We will never be perfect in this life, but God is committed to continue to work in us to change us and make us better; more like Jesus. As we have discussed, this process of "sanctification" goes on our entire earthly life.

When God is working on us, especially on a behavior or stronghold that is deeply rooted, He may have to get our attention through circumstances or events. If we resist, this process can be painful. The painful part comes when we realize the effect we may have had on others, especially those we love.

So, whether our trials and tribulations are because of satanic attack, opposition, bad decisions, God trying to change something in our life, or God working to change our heart, we need to seek Him for understanding. If we do not seek Him, we can end up confused and disillusioned. We need to open our hearts to Him, to hear what He is saying and co-operate with what He wants to do. God always has a way out of difficult times. We can grow and become stronger during these times and deepen our relationship with God. He is always ready to help us.

QUESTIONS FOR REFLECTION AND DISCUSSION

1. Are you experiencing a difficult time in your life? In what way(s)? Have you been seeking God for understanding? If so, what do You sense Him telling you *about you*?

   _____

   _____

   _____

   _____

2. As God begins to reveal to you what you are going through and why, what action steps come to mind? Write them below. (You may want to share these with another person and ask him or her to hold you accountable to following through with them.)

   _____

   _____

   _____

   _____

3. If you are praying and seeking the Lord about your circumstances and don't feel you yet understand what is going on, what should be your next step?

   _____

   _____

   _____

   _____

TAKE A KNEE

"Dear Father, I realize trials will come in life and I need to trust You during difficult times. I also realize You want to give me the understanding I need. Thank You that You are always with me. I ask You to be my helper and give me the grace and strength I need. I praise You for all of Your goodness and love for me. I thank You that having victory over all difficult times will come. You are faithful to always be with me and near me."

Chapter 6

PRAYER AND FASTING

Many churches do not teach on fasting. Yet the Bible has much to say about this. As you read the Bible, you will find many examples of people fasting in order to seek God for various reasons. Daniel, David, Nehemiah, Ezekiel, Jeremiah, Jehoshaphat, and others in the Old Testament sought God through prayer and fasting. In the New Testament, the apostles Paul and John, as well as Jesus Himself, are among those who took time for prayer and fasting. So what is fasting, and why should we do it?

Fasting is simply not eating for a period of time. The Bible gives examples of people fasting from one day to forty days. Jesus fasted for forty days in the wilderness. The Bible states that *"Jesus was led up by the Spirit into the wilderness to be tempted by the devil"* (Matthew 4:1). Since God cannot tempt anyone with evil (see James 1:13), the Bible is stating what happened to Jesus when

He fasted: He was tempted by Satan when he was weak physically from fasting and overcame the temptations by trusting God and fighting Satan with the words of God.

Isaiah 58 also speaks about fasting. It states that the purpose of fasting is to seek God and to gain new freedom in our lives. The purpose of a fast is not only to humble oneself before the Lord, but also to *"loose the bonds of wickedness, to undo the straps of the yoke, to let the oppressed go free, and to break every yoke"* (Isaiah 58:6). This scripture states that God's desire is to raise us up and break bonds on our life. He wants us to experience freedom so we can live the life He has for us.

Fasting allows us to seek God's truth and gain insight into His will and purpose for us. The purpose is not just to abase ourselves. It is to humbly seek God and ask for His will to be known to us. When we fast, we are denying our body food and our spiritual senses are heightened. This allows us to seek God and get insight into His will. We are desiring to know more deeply His truth and how to apply it. We fast to break bondage in our lives and in others' lives. We also fast and pray to seek God for our family, those we know, and our nation and its leaders. God honors our time set aside for fasting.

Fasting isn't just about giving up food, although fasting alone can give physical benefits, such as purging the body of toxins. Fasting is meant to be used with prayer—meaning we are to set aside time to seek the Lord's insight, truth, and direction. We are focusing on seeking God, shutting out other distracting things as best we can, and hearing from Him.

If you have to work on a day or time you set aside to fast, you can pray as you go about your tasks or set aside lunchtime to not eat but to get alone and pray.

Fasting can also be used as a form of repentance. In the Bible, there are cases where people fasted to repent of their sins and ask for God's favor to come back upon them. After his sin with Bathsheba and Uriah, David fasted, prayed, and sought God for His favor and for forgiveness for his sin and for the life of his child (see 2 Samuel 12:15-23).

Some reasons to fast and pray include:

1. To seek God for answers and direction
2. To humble oneself before God
3. To repent for sin for ourself, for others, or for our nation
4. To get greater insight and revelation into God's Word and truth
5. To draw closer to God
6. To break bondage in our life, other's lives, or in our nation

We do not have to fast for God to hear us. He is always there and always with us as His children. But when our spirit is troubled or confused, we can draw close to God through prayer and fasting. God knows our heart, and if we are crying out to Him, He hears us and will answer us. The book of James states, *"If any of you lacks wisdom, let him ask God, who gives generously to all without reproach, and it will be given him"* (James 1:5).

God wants us to hear from him and know His will. He wants to give us direction and understanding. His presence is with us continually through His Holy Spirit. So we don't have to fast for God to hear us. We fast to draw closer to God, to deny the body of food so we are more sensitive to God's Spirit, and to hear Him speak to our hearts.

A typical fast is for one to several days and is accompanied with prayer for the purpose of seeking God. But there are different types of fasts found in Scripture:

1. The first type is when we fast from all foods but still drink water, since the body can only go for a limited time without water.

2. The second fast is listed in Daniel and known as the "Daniel Fast." It is not eating any desirable foods and regularly seeking God (see Daniel 9). Daniel had important duties and had to continue to work. So he ate foods to give him strength but denied himself of desirable foods for several weeks.
3. A third type of fast is one that lasts one to three days where neither food nor water is consumed. This took place in Esther 4 to seek God's favor and reverse evil decrees against the Jews.
4. The fourth type of fast is a 40-day fast. God called Moses and Jesus to fast for 40 days for His purpose. Moses did this twice in Exodus, and Jesus did it in the New Testament (see Matthew 4). Going without water for 40 days is not possible, and therefore it was miraculous that Moses was able to do so.

In my life, I have gained many insights into God's Word and His will for me while praying and fasting. One time as I was praying and fasting, God spoke to my heart and said to me, "Do you want to see what I can do, or do you want to just experience what you can do?" This was a shocker to me, and I said, "Yes, I want to see what you desire to do through me."

God works through people. His anointing, or enabling of us to accomplish His desires, flows through people. God gives us tasks to do and wants to empower us to do them. When we fast and pray to seek and hear Him, He reveals to us His desire to work through us to accomplish things in this life. God is looking for those with an open heart, a willing heart, a heart after Him. Our heart, as the Bible speaks of it, is our desire center. We look at the outside of people, but God looks at the heart (see 1 Samuel 16:7). He desires to work through us, and as we seek Him, He will change our heart and renew our minds so that they line up with His desires for us.

The Bible says we are to be renewed in our thinking and be transformed by a renewed mind: *"Do not be conformed to this world, but be transformed by the renewal of your mind, that by testing you may discern what is the will of God, what is good and acceptable and perfect"* (Romans 12:2). We also are told *"to put off your old self, which belongs to your former manner of life and is corrupt through deceitful desires, and* **to be renewed in the spirit of your minds**, *and to put on the new self, created after the likeness of God in true righteousness and holiness"* (Ephesians 4:22-24, emphasis added).

God wants to change the way we think and live our lives. Our "stinking thinking" corrupts our life and keeps us from all God has for us. As our thinking changes, our heart changes. And as we enter times of prayer and fasting, we set aside time to allow God to minister His truth to us and renew us. We don't have to fast for this to happen. But fasting does help us to crowd out the disturbances of life and get quiet before God so we can allow Him to work in our life. Again, we don't have to fast to hear from God or for Him to work in our life. Times of fasting just help facilitate this. It can quiet our spirit so fellowship with Him takes place and opens us up to hear Him or be ministered to by His Word.

Released Into Ministry

Acts 13 tells how there were church leaders in Antioch who were fasting, praying, and seeking God. During this time, the Holy Spirit told them Barnabas and Paul were to be released to do the ministry God had called them to. So the leaders laid their hands on them, prayed for them, and sent them out to do the ministry they were called to. God spoke to this group in their spirits as they were fasting and praying, sensitive to God's Spirit. His instructions were given to release Paul and Barnabas into special ministry.

God honors us seeking Him. In the case of Paul and Barnabas, He spoke direction. Many are called to ministry as they seek God with prayer and fasting. We are all called to be God's ministers where we are. But some are called to go out to fulfill the call of God on their life in special ways.

God wants to break any and all bondage in our life due to wrong thinking. Seek Him for His truth, and He will reveal it.

Physical Issues

I realize that some people have genuine physical issues with fasting. A man with Type 2 diabetes told me recently that he was unable to go on a complete fast with no food but could drink some juices during the fast to keep his blood sugar at the proper level. If you have some genuine physical issues, perhaps consulting your doctor about fasting would be in order. I am not a doctor and do not know all of the proper issues concerning this. Be wise in your decisions.

Fasting Things Besides Food

I have spoken to some who have told me they have fasted from watching TV or denying other types of things and have considered that their fast. I think that denying yourself those things and instead spending time in prayer, Bible reading, and seeking God has genuine value. Any time we set aside time to seek God instead of pursuing other activities is time well spent. However, denying those things is not true fasting, which means refraining from eating specifically. It's worth it for all of us to truly fast from food and seek God.

QUESTIONS FOR REFLECTION AND DISCUSSION

1. Have you ever set aside time for prayer and fasting?

   _____
   _____
   _____

2. Do you think you should set aside time to do this?

   _____
   _____
   _____
   _____

3. Do you have things on your heart that you need to seek God about for which fasting with prayer might be appropriate?

   _____
   _____
   _____
   _____

TAKE A KNEE

Let's pray. "Father, I know I need to hear from you about my life and hear what you desire to say to me. I trust You to lead me to fast as I need to and You desire me to. I am in Your hands and am Your servant."

A FINAL WORD

Seeking God is more than an ideal; it is a real necessity in our life. As we pursue God, we will discover His purpose for us and He will make Himself known to us. He wants to change our hearts, renew our minds, and heal our souls. He wants us to be whole and have joy and peace deep within us, sharing it with others.

God desires to reveal Himself to us and establish His relationship with us. We become His child when we accept Christ into our life. Then, it becomes our responsibility to pursue Him and develop a pattern of discipline to set aside time daily to know Him deeper. As we do this, He responds to us and reveals Himself to us in an even greater way.

Is seeking God crucial to our lives? Absolutely. We all have a deep, inner need to know Him and receive from Him all He has for us. Seeking God, pursuing Him, and running hard toward Him, all result in our lives being an adventure, one of discovering the One who truly loves us and has good purposes for our life.

I hope you will embrace this adventure—of seeking God, of finding Him, and of being transformed into all He designed for you to be!

ABOUT THE AUTHOR

Lou Turner wrote *Living Life God's Way* out of his passion for men to discover God, and to get to know Him and what He has for them. This 13-book series is the culmination of Lou's own journey—a life of seeking God, studying His Word, memorizing Scripture and meditating on it, and practical experience with family, community, marketplace work, and Christian ministry. It also comes, by Lou's own admission, from life experiences of both successes and mistakes, as a result of both good and bad decisions.

Lou has headed ministries, written and taught workshops, classes, and seminars, and discipled dozens of men. Now, he has put into print the things he has learned to help other men along their path and journey.

Most of Lou's growing up years were spent in Detroit and its suburbs, where he was raised in a pastor's home. Following his graduation from university with a Bachelor of Science in Business Administration, Lou and his wife planted and pastored a church for three years. After that time, he felt the strong call of God to return to business.

Over the years, Lou has served in numerous senior executive positions with national and international companies in the real estate and oil and gas industries. As of this writing, Lou is still active in business with his own home building company. He has been married to his wife Joan since they were 20. They have three children and 10 grandchildren and make their home in Phoenix, Arizona.

www.ingramcontent.com/pod-product-compliance
Lightning Source LLC
Chambersburg PA
CBHW021121080526
44587CB00010B/596